Animal Cousins

by Gail Blasser Riley · illustrated by Jennifer DiRubbio

Scott Foresman

Editorial Offices: Glenview, Illinois • New York, New York
Sales Offices: Reading, Massachusetts • Duluth, Georgia
Glenview, Illinois • Carrollton, Texas • Menlo Park, California

Have you ever seen an armadillo?
If not, perhaps someday you will see
one. An armadillo has claws on its
toes. It also has a long, thin tongue.
An armadillo is about two feet long.

Could an armadillo grow as long as a car? Not today!

But millions of years ago, a cousin of the armadillo lived on Earth. This animal was the glyptodont (GLIP-toh-dont).

How big was this animal? About fourteen feet long! That is about as long as a car.

Many other animals lived at the
same time. Most of them are not here
anymore.

Some of them still live today. Giraffes and elephants lived at that time. So did pigs and deer.

The armadillo eats insects and
worms. Bugs stick to its long tongue.
Look at all those bugs!

Did the glyptodont eat the same things? It may have. Can you guess how long its tongue was? Very, very long!

Like all animals, the glyptodont tried
not to get hurt. Walking near an enemy
could be a big mistake!

thylacosmilus

One enemy looked like a lion. But it was much, much bigger! It had long, sharp teeth and claws.

How did a glyptodont protect itself?
Look at the hard shell on the armadillo.
It is like a big helmet. It is hard as stone.
An armadillo can roll up inside the shell.

The glyptodont had this helmet too.
It could roll up inside its shell too.

It also had a tail with big, sharp
points on the end. No one would want
to be near this tail!

Why don't we see glyptodonts
today? It is all because of the weather.

The Earth got too cold.
Glyptodonts could not live in ice
and snow. All of them died.

So, when you meet an armadillo, think of its cousin, the glyptodont. And remember an animal that lived long, long ago—before there were any people on Earth!